Portrait of
EDMONTON
& NORTHERN ALBERTA

Photographs by Andrew Bradley
Text by Jennifer Groundwater

Altitude Publishing
The Canadian Rockies / Victoria
www.altitudepublishing.com

PORTRAIT OF EDMONTON & NORTHERN ALBERTA

Photographs copyright 2004© Andrew Bradley
Text copyright 2004© Jennifer Groundwater
All rights reserved. No part of this book may be reproduced in any form
or by any means, electronic, mechanical or digital, without prior
written permission from the Publisher.

National Library of Canada Cataloguing in Publication
Bradley, Andrew, 1962-

Portrait of Edmonton and northern Alberta / Andrew Bradley,
photographer ; Jennifer Groundwater, author.

(Altitude portrait book)
ISBN 1-55153-221-2 (pbk.)

1. Edmonton (Alta.)--Pictorial works.   2. Alberta, Northern--
Pictorial works. I. Groundwater, Jennifer II. Title. III. Series.

FC3694.4.B73 2004   971.23'3403'0222   C2004-901139-1

We acknowledge the financial support of the Government of Canada
through the Book Publishing Industry Development Program (BPIDP)
for our publishing activities.

Layout/design: Scott Manktelow
Editor: Kara Turner

Altitude Publishing Canada Ltd.
The Canadian Rockies / Victoria
Head office: 1500 Railway Avenue,
Canmore, Alberta T1W 1P6
1-800-957-6888

www.altitudepublishing.com

Front cover: Downtown Edmonton from the Muttart Conservatory
Back cover paperback: Aerial view in autumn near Fort McMurray
Frontispiece: Alberta Legislature building
This page: Downtown Edmonton reflected in the North
Saskatchewan River
Opposite page: Fort McMurray on the Athabasca River

Printed in Canada by Friesen Printers

Altitude GreenTree Program
Altitude will plant two trees for every tree used in the production of
this book.

TABLE OF CONTENTS

INTRODUCTION

In the minds of most Albertans, "Northern Alberta" begins just beyond the city limits of Edmonton, the provincial capital. In fact, Edmonton is still in the southern half of the province. North of the capital, a vast area stretches all the way to the Northwest Territories, encompassing wide swathes of boreal forest, huge oil and gas reserves, pristine lakes, and very few population centres. Visitors to the area may come for the abundant hunting and fishing opportunities, to view the northern lights, or to participate in the oil and gas industry.

Edmonton is the gateway to this beautiful area, but is also a compelling destination in its own right. Located on the banks of the North Saskatchewan River, the city, which celebrates its centennial in 2004, today is home to well over half a million people. Alberta's capital is known as the Festival City for the wealth of major festivals that take place here every year. It is also known to shopping aficionados the world over as the home of the West Edmonton Mall, the planet's largest shopping and entertainment complex.

Edmonton had its origins as a Hudson's Bay Company fur trading post, established in 1795. The native groups who were already living in the area at the time traded their abundant furs with the European settlers for other goods. Gradually the settlement grew until the Klondike Gold Rush of 1897-98, which swelled the population of the fledgling city. Today Edmonton's fortunes are more closely allied with oil and gas extraction than with gold prospecting. In 1947, oil was found just south of Edmonton, in Leduc. This discovery changed the fortunes of the province, which is now thought to have one-third of the world's oil reserves, and of Edmonton along with it. It is now a comfortable city whose residents enjoy the largest urban parkland system in North America, stretching along the North Saskatchewan River Valley for dozens of kilometres.

Edmontonians are known to love hockey. Outdoor rinks appear every winter to indulge this passion in its purest form. Edmonton is also known as the city of the greatest hockey player ever, Wayne Gretzky, who shot to worldwide fame as a member of the Edmonton Oilers in the 1980s. Edmonton's long winters also provide frequent cultural distractions in the way of the arts, including theatre, dance and music. There are excellent venues around the city hosting these events, and there is always something going on. CKUA, the oldest public radio broadcaster in Canada, is headqurtered in Edmonton, and offers outstanding programming and news on the events in the capital and around the province. In summer, Edmontonians shed their layers of warm clothing to enjoy the abundant green space, dozens of golf courses, cycling, running, and rollerblading on the river trails, and a wealth of major festivals. There is a festival of some kind taking place just about every summer weekend. Jazz and blues, folk music, the Fringe, comedy, Shakespeare, Heritage, and many others are celebrated in various parks around the city. Summer in Edmonton can be one long party, especially since the city's northern location means that the twilights go on seemingly forever. Sunset happens well after 10 pm in June and July.

Heading out of Edmonton in any direction, the views become more expansive as the towns grow smaller. The communities of the north are diverse in nature. Many are ranching and farming communities, like Peace River. Some, such as Fort McMurray, are almost entirely devoted to the extraction of oil and gas. Lac La Biche is known for its freshwater fishery as well as forestry and the oil industry. Grande Prairie's economy is based on a mix of forestry, oil and gas, and farming. Many Northern Alberta communities are developing a tourism focus, capitalizing on their abundant natural attractions to entice visitors with an appreciation for unspoiled wilderness. The list of outdoor activities available is almost endless — there are even white sand beaches and warm lakes to enjoy.

While most Albertans are familiar with Edmonton, Northern Alberta remains unknown to many residents of the southern part of the province. As the photographs in this book show, Northern Alberta is more than worthy of discovery. Full of history, bursting with contemporary energy, and offering an expanse of the great outdoors, Northern Alberta is a very special part of an exceptional province.

Opposite Page: Aerial view of Edmonton and the North Saskatchewan River Valley.

EDMONTON

Top: Edmonton's city lights reflect in the dusky North Saskatchewan River.

Bottom: Edmonton's modern downtown continues to soar skyward as the city's fortunes grow, but there is still plenty of green space to keep the city in balance.

Top: From the air, it is easy to see the importance of the North Saskatchewan River to the city. In days past it was a vital transportation route. Today, the green spaces along the river are the lungs of the city.

Bottom: In summer, commercial jet boat tours offer a new way to look at the city — from the water. The North Saskatchewan is quite shallow as it passes through Edmonton, so a jet boat, with its exceptionally shallow draft, is the ideal craft for navigating the water. Emergency crews also use the river as an alternate to roads.

Top: A scenic nighttime view of Edmonton.

Middle: This sign welcomes visitors to Edmonton at Gateway Park, where there is also a visitor information centre and an interpretive display about the oil industry.

Bottom: Edmonton's parks and public spaces have plenty of whimsical art, like this downtown sculpture that celebrates the performing arts.

Opposite top: Edmonton on a sunny summer day is a beautiful place to be.

Opposite Middle: A close up look at the oil derrick that greets visitors at the southern gateway to Edmonton. It is a replica of the original Imperial Oil derrick #1 in Leduc (south of Edmonton, where oil was found in 1947) and commemorates the early days of oil exploration in Alberta.

Opposite Bottom: Edmonton's downtown skyline, with the venerable Fairmont Hotel Macdonald at the left.

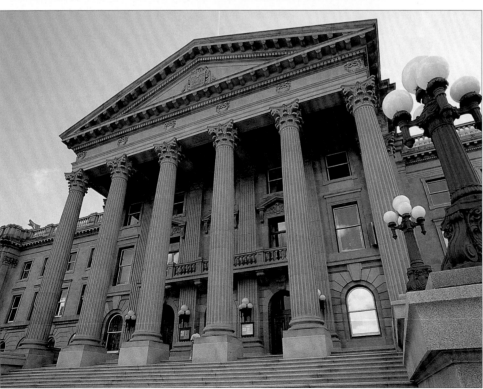

Top: Alberta's Legislature Building is one of Edmonton's most beautiful downtown landmarks. The reflecting pools become skating rinks in the wintertime, while in summer they complement the colourful flower gardens that adorn the grounds.

Bottom: Completed in 1912 in the Beaux-Arts style, built of granite and sandstone, the provincial Legislature Building sits near the original site of Fort Edmonton.

Opposite: The Legislature Building took 5 years to complete. The rotunda is built of marble and each of the solid marble pillars weighs 16 tonnes.

Top: Grant McEwan College offers a wide range of career and university programs at its four campuses located throughout Edmonton. Pictured here is the downtown campus, a landmark with its distinctive modern design. The college was named for the former Lieutenant Governor of Alberta, the Honourable J.W. Grant McEwan.

Bottom: A look up at the towers of the downtown campus.

Opposite top: Edmonton's modern and airy city hall was built in 1992. Located in the heart of downtown, opposite Winston Churchill Square, city hall features a striking glass pyramid and a bell tower with a 99-tune carillon. The reflecting pool and fountains are a pleasant place for a summer lunch al fresco.

Opposite bottom left: Cyclists are a common sight on Edmonton's bridges and riverside paths.

Opposite bottom right: Edmonton's skyscrapers reflect more than each other — their very presence reflects the prosperity that the discovery of oil brought to the city.

West Edmonton Mall is without doubt Edmonton's biggest visitor attraction. Covering the equivalent of 48 city blocks, the mall features over 800 stores and many major attractions, in addition to over 110 eating establishments.

Top: Bourbon Street evokes the spirit of New Orleans, offering over a dozen places to eat, drink and be merry.

Bottom: The Ice Palace is busy all day long with skaters practicing their figure skating moves or just serenely circling the ice. Sometimes the Edmonton Oilers hockey team takes to the NHL-sized ice for practice.

Top: The World Waterpark offers over 5 acres of watery fun for families and thrill seekers alike. The temperature is always balmy under the glass roof, and there are activities for everyone from babies to bungy jumpers.

Bottom: Europa Boulevard is designed to remind visitors of a Continental European street. It features smaller, more intimate shops and faux-old building fronts — the overall effect is charming.

Following page top inset: Having a whale of a time at West Ed!

Following page middle inset: Mardi Gras figureheads keep watch over Bourbon Street.

Following page bottom inset: The World Waterpark is a great place to make a splash.

Following pages main photo: The life-size replica of Columbus' ship Santa Maria dominates the water, but this area of the mall also features a submarine ride and other attractions.

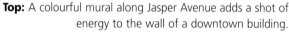

Top: A colourful mural along Jasper Avenue adds a shot of energy to the wall of a downtown building.

Bottom: You never know where a beautiful piece of public art will surprise you in Edmonton. This bronze family can be found near the Legislature Building.

Opposite top: A federal government building — in this case Canada Place — can indeed be a thing of beauty when seen from the right angle.

Opposite bottom left: A closer look at this mural gives a sense of stepping into the past. The mural is opposite the building that houses the High Level Streetcar in Old Strathcona.

Opposite bottom right: This imaginatively-designed building in Coronation Park houses an Olympic-sized pool, a perfect place for a dip after a visit to the nearby Odyssium or a stroll among the flower gardens on the grounds.

Top: Whatever the season, there is always a spectacular thematic display in the Show Pyramid at the Muttart Conservatory. Not surprisingly, this is a popular place for wedding photos.

Bottom: The Arid Pyramid features the harsh and serene beauty of succulents and other desert plants.

Opposite: The distinctive glass pyramids of the Muttart Conservatory are an Edmonton landmark. The four pyramids house separate gardens, each with its own theme: Arid, Temperate, Tropical, and a Show pyramid with frequently changing displays. Muttart in winter is an excellent escape from the chilly weather, while in summer the outdoor gardens are an added draw.

It's easy to spend an afternoon gazing at the more than 700 species of plants on display in Muttart's gardens. It's impossible for a photographer to resist the patterns and colours found here, whether in a bank of annuals or a single leaf.

Top: The Temperate Pyramid features a delightful abundance of native plants in a tranquil atmosphere.

Bottom: A young visitor uses all her senses to experience Muttart.

Opposite, clockwise from top left: Detail from the Arid Pyramid, a fan-shaped frond bursts with green, a delicate indoor spring collage, outdoor banks overflow with colour.

Top: The Provincial Museum of Alberta offers exciting glimpses into Alberta's natural and social history, as well as offering contemporary displays on aboriginal culture and the environment. Pictured here is the Natural History Gallery, featuring fossils, gold and gemstones, live bugs and stuffed birds.

Bottom: The exterior of the Provincial Museum of Alberta is almost as interesting as the interior. Visitors can stroll the trails, enjoy the views over the river valley, and admire the art on the outdoor walls.

Opposite top: Edmonton is home to Alberta's Aviation Museum, which features a number of restored and replica aircraft, including this Westland Lysander.

Opposite bottom: The Valley Zoo in Edmonton is home to more than 100 species of animal, including meerkats **(left)** and zebras **(right).** The zoo is open year-round and offers numerous interpretive programs.

Top left: Edmonton has a large Ukrainian population, whose roots in the province stretch back over 100 years.

Top Right: St. Josaphat Ukrainian Catholic Cathedral is one of Edmonton's most picturesque buildings, with a magnificent interior to match its handsome exterior.

Bottom: The interior of the church at the Ukrainian Cultural Heritage Village just outside Edmonton.

Opposite: Edmonton's Odyssium is a museum where kids (and grown-ups) can learn about the world and the universe. The hands-on galleries offer many opportunities to learn while having fun. Pictured is the Body Fantastic Gallery **(top)**; the exterior of the museum, designed by Douglas J. Cardinal **(bottom left)**; and the Zeiss Star Projector, nicknamed "Sophie", in the Margaret Zeidler Star Theatre **(bottom right).**

Fort Edmonton Park is where the history of the city is brought vividly to life by costumed interpreters. The park is set out in various streets, each of which evokes a particular period in Edmonton's history. The Hudson's Bay Fort **(top, and opposite top)** recreates the fur trade era circa the mid-1840s. 1885 Street shows Edmonton as a frontier town, complete with saloon, millinery, and blacksmith shop **(opposite, bottom right),** but fur was still important **(opposite, bottom left).** In 1905 Street, the new respectability of Edmonton as the capital of the new province of Alberta is highlighted **(bottom left).** 1920 Street shows what life was like for Edmontonians during the Roaring 20s. Visitors can ride the steam train, stagecoach and streetcars in the various streets.

Top: Edmonton's Flatiron Building was erected in 1913 on Jasper Avenue by a speculator named William Gibson (hence the building's other name, the Gibson Block). The triangular design echoes that of the more famous Flatiron Building in New York City and is unusual in Alberta architecture. Originally a commercial building, the Gibson Block eventually became a rooming house and was closed in the 1970s, then slated for demolition in 1993. Fortunately, the historic and architectural value of the building was recognized, and it was restored. It currently houses an emergency shelter for women.

Bottom: An interesting juxtaposition of old and new architecture in downtown Edmonton.

Klondike Days is Edmonton's signature event — 10 days in July devoted to celebrating the excitement of the Klondike gold rush days. Much of the action takes place at Northlands Park, but there are events all through the city for the 10 days. Pancake breakfasts, bathtub races through city streets, concerts and performances all day long give the downtown a carnival atmosphere. At Northlands, there is an agricultural display, an extensive midway, a casino, and chuckwagon races. There is even a race for homemade rafts down the North Saskatchewan River.

Top: The RCMP always participate in the annual Klondike Days Parade, which draws over 190,000 spectators to kick off the festivities.

Bottom: Marching bands are a popular element of the Klondike Days Parade.

Northlands Park is packed with people during Klondike Days. The midway is one of North America's largest, and there are numerous other activities to enjoy as well **(top and bottom),** including the Family Fun Zone, various marketplaces, and Bonanza Park, a recreation of the gold mining era. During the course of the 10 days, over three quarters of a million people come through the gates.

Opposite top: The Klondike Chuckwagon Derby offers a rich purse for the fastest teams. The race is a highlight of the yearly calendar of the World Professional Chuckwagon Association, and the event gets pulses racing.

Opposite bottom left: Period costumes add even more colour to Klondike Days.

Opposite bottom right: Panning for gold at the Chilkoot Gold Mine in Bonanza Park. This area of Klondike Days offers a recreation of the gold mining era and a chance to pan for gold like an old-time miner.

Top: Commonwealth Stadium is home to the Edmonton Eskimos football team, and plays host to numerous national and international sporting events. The original stadium was built in 1978 when Edmonton hosted the Commonwealth Games, and it is still one of the largest stadia in Canada — the only one of its size with real grass.

Bottom: Edmonton is also known as the "City of Champions", and this piece of public art along the Kingsway celebrates the hometown athletes who make the city proud.

Opposite top: Edmonton's Folk Music Festival lights up Gallagher Park with the city as a glittering backdrop. The four-day Folk Festival takes place every August and is considered one of the finest in North America, with artists from every musical genre performing.

Opposite bottom left and right: The only rule at Edmonton's Fringe Festival is that anything goes, which makes for some exciting theatrical moments over the 11 lively days in August when the Festival takes place. Old Strathcona plays host to the festival, which besides theatre features plenty of free family entertainment and musical performances.

Old Strathcona is one of Edmonton's most compelling neighbourhoods, with turn-of-the-century architecture housing funky shops and restaurants. It's the artsy heart of the city and an area that visitors love to discover. The historic tram pictured here **(top left and bottom)** runs from Old Strathcona over the High Level Bridge daily in summer — a wonderful trip back into Edmonton's past. The Old Strathcona Farmers' Market is also home to this lifelike statue **(top right)** commemorating the eight Alberta firefighters killed in the line of duty in the city in the 20th century.

The Fairmont Hotel Macdonald **(top),** now an Edmonton landmark, began life in 1915 as the Grand Trunk Pacific Hotel. Despite its handsome appearance and commanding location high above the river, the hotel fell on tough times in the mid-1980s and was slated for demolition. Fortunately it was designated a heritage building and was lovingly restored after its purchase by Canadian Pacific Hotels (now Fairmont). Since its re-opening in 1991, the hotel has come to stand for elegance and luxury for visitors to the heart of Edmonton. The interior of the hotel includes the clubby Confederation Lounge with its scenic river views **(bottom).**

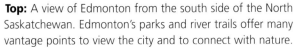

Top: A view of Edmonton from the south side of the North Saskatchewan. Edmonton's parks and river trails offer many vantage points to view the city and to connect with nature.

Bottom: *The Edmonton Queen* riverboat offers a popular cruise along the North Saskatchewan River. Visitors set sail opposite the Hotel Macdonald at Rafter's Landing and enjoy a leisurely voyage along the river, along with a meal and drinks.

Opposite top: The University of Alberta is in the foreground of this aerial view of Edmonton. It is one of Canada's foremost research universities and has over 30,000 students.

Opposite bottom left: Government House was established in 1913 as the official residence for the Lieutenant Governor of Alberta, but it was used in this capacity for a mere 25 years. Located next to the Provincial Museum of Alberta, it is now used for conferences and special events. Members of the public are welcome to visit on Sundays.

Opposite bottom right: The colourful Chinatown Gate welcomes visitors to Edmonton's Chinatown. It was built to commemorate Edmonton's relationship with its twin city, Harbin.

Top: Edmonton under a flawless blue sky.

Bottom: This lively piece of art, titled "Recycles", can be found in downtown Edmonton in Beaver Hills House Park. The five bicycles are made of found iron objects and can be pedalled by passers-by.

Opposite: *The Edmonton Queen* riverboat floats along the North Saskatchewan River into the reflected city skyline.

Located just north of Edmonton, St. Albert was originally founded as a Catholic Oblate mission, which attracted many Métis and francophone settlers. Today the city remains proud of its French roots. St. Albert Place **(top and bottom)** is home to the city's administration and elected officials, but is also a focal point for community activities. Its sinewy lines are easily recognizable as the work of noted Canadian architect Douglas Cardinal (himself of Métis heritage). St. Albert Place is home to the Arden Theatre, a well-loved hall for musical and theatrical performances, the local library, and the Musée Heritage Museum. It also features public art such as this whimsical sculpture **(opposite top).**

Opposite top right: The Vital Grandin Centre museum offers insight into the early days of the Catholic mission in St. Albert.

Opposite bottom left: Built in 1861 by Father Albert Lacombe (St. Albert's namesake) and some Métis followers, the simple Father Lacombe Chapel is the oldest log building in Alberta. Father Lacombe and Bishop Vital Grandin are buried here.

Opposite bottom right: Hole's Greenhouses and Gardens in St. Albert is one of the most colourful places to visit in the Edmonton area, especially in spring and early summer.

NORTHERN ALBERTA

Northern Alberta begins where Edmonton and area ends — a vast wilderness with some cities and towns here and there. There is a vibrant life to these destinations of the north, including Lac La Biche, Slave Lake, Fort McMurray, Peace River, and Grande Prairie. For many people, Northern Alberta represents unspoiled wilderness of the kind that is in short supply elsewhere in the world.

Top: The waterways of northern Alberta offer incredible vistas and opportunities for paddling and camping in serene solitude.

Bottom: The communities in Northern Alberta, like elsewhere in the province, are frequently a melting pot of nationalities from all over the world. Russian, Ukrainian, French, Métis, and many others share their heritage with their neighbours and visitors.

Opposite: A solitary farmhouse under dramatic skies.

Top: Vegreville, just east of Edmonton, is home to the world's largest Pysanka (Ukrainian Easter egg). It was conceived as a tribute to the RCMP in its centennial year, 1974. The various colours and patterns on the egg represent prosperity, life, good fortune, a good harvest, protection and security, and eternity.

Bottom: Many Albertans revel in their rich Ukrainian heritage, whether it be cooking special meals, participating in Ukrainian dancing, or collecting colourful trinkets.

Opposite: Frost heaves and a winter sunset make for uncommon beauty on frozen Lac La Biche.

Top: Northern Alberta is one of the finest places in the world to view the aurora borealis, or northern lights. These colours are most frequently seen in winter months, dancing across the night sky and creating moving patterns and bands of light. The most common colour is green, but often red, orange or pink can be seen as well. The northern lights are a truly unforgettable sight.

Bottom: Alberta is a relatively young province (celebrating its centennial in 2005) but some of its buildings evoke a strong sense of a forgotten past.

Top: Scenery and solitude are two of the reasons to spend time in Northern Alberta, whatever the season.

Bottom: On the shores of Lac La Biche is the David Thompson statue, built in 1999 in honour of the famous mapmaker and explorer. Thompson arrived in the area in 1798 as part of his prodigious exploration of the north and west portion of North America. Ironically, the statue is not a true likeness of David Thompson, since no portrait is known to exist of this incredible explorer.

Alberta's native peoples celebrate their traditions at powwows held during the summer months. The powwow is a chance to reconnect with one another, to the earth and with native spirituality. For non-natives, powwows offer the chance to learn more about the traditions, music and dance of Canada's First Nations. Some powwows are competitive events where prize money is awarded to the best drummers and dancers, but all are social gatherings where families and friends enjoy time together.

Top left: Each teepee's design has symbolic meaning to the owner.

Top right: A young native dancer dressed in traditional regalia.

Bottom: Drummers setting a rhythm for dancers at a powwow.

Opposite: A dancer in tribal regalia is alive with colour and motion.

Fort McMurray is a booming town of about 60,000 souls located in northeastern Alberta. It is a town based on oil extraction, yet surrounded by thousands of hectares of pristine boreal forest. Located at the confluence of four rivers, Fort McMurray offers excellent opportunities for the outdoor enthusiast.

Top: A spectacular moon rises over downtown Fort McMurray.

Bottom: A Fort McMurray neighbourhood becomes a geometrical abstraction from the air.

Opposite top: Fort McMurray's City Hall.

Opposite bottom left: This siltstone sculpture of wood bison welcomes visitors to Syncrude's Wood Bison Trail.

Opposite bottom right: Historic buildings bear witness to the past at Fort McMurray's Heritage Park.

The Fort McMurray area sits on an enormous deposit of oil sand — the largest known oil deposit in the world — known as the Athabasca Oil Sands. The economy of the city is almost entirely driven by oil extraction and refining by the two major employers, Syncrude and Suncor. Bitumen is extracted from the sand and processed into a higher-grade light crude oil.

Top: A service truck rests under the arm of a massive hydraulic shovel at Syncrude Canada Ltd.'s North Mine. The shovel, which digs oil sand year round, has a bucket that is approximately the size of a double-car garage.

Bottom: One of the original bucketwheel reclaimers (foreground) and a dragline sit on display at the Oil Sands Discovery Centre in Fort McMurray.

Opposite: Control towers and conveyors, hard at work moving oil sand into windrows, are silhouetted against a northern sunset **(top left).** Close-up of an oil-sand encrusted bucketwheel reclaimer, which scoops piles of oil sand onto conveyors **(top right).** A gigantic heavy hauler dwarfs a Syncrude employee **(bottom right).** A bucketwheel reclaimer in Syncrude's East Mine, placing oil sand onto conveyor belts **(bottom left).**

Top: Bush planes provide the fastest means of access to many rivers and lakes in Northern Alberta.

Bottom: Bison are making a comeback in their namesake region of Wood Buffalo, which surrounds Fort McMurray. Although native to the region, these immense animals were in danger of dying out completely. In 1993, 30 buffalo were moved to the Syncrude site and encouraged to range over the reclaimed grasslands. The area is now home to a thriving buffalo herd, thanks to this joint effort by Syncrude and the Fort McKay First Nation.

Opposite: A stunning aerial view of a Northern Alberta forest and river.

Top: Grande Prairie Regional College nestles into the Bear Creek valley at twilight. The college offers university-transfer programs, college diplomas and continuing education courses in a wide range of subjects.

Bottom: Grain elevators in Sexsmith, north of Grande Prairie, stand as graceful testaments to the agricultural economy of the Peace Country. Grain elevators such as these were built in the thousands across western Canada between the 1890s and the 1930s. Today these wooden sentinels gradually are being replaced by more utilitarian steel elevators.

Top: Grande Prairie Regional College was the first major project designed by now-renowned architect Douglas Cardinal. Its undulating lines foreshadow many of his future buildings, such as the Canadian Museum of Civilization in Hull.

Bottom: One of Grande Prairie's prettiest buildings is known as Centre 2000. Inside, the Grande Prairie Museum offers visitors a trip through time, from the dinosaurs through Grande Prairie's human history to the present day.

Like many Northern Alberta towns, Peace River began as a fur-trading fort. It was settled first by missionaries and later on by farming settlers. It is located in a rich agricultural area and today is a trade centre for a large surrounding area.

Top: The confluence of the Smokey and Peace Rivers as seen from Twelve Foot Davis' (see below) gravesite.

Bottom: The Peace River bridge.

Opposite top: Peace River's picturesque former train station now serves as the tourist information centre.

Opposite bottom left: "Twelve Foot" Davis was the most famous inhabitant of Peace River. H. F. Davis was not particularly tall — his nickname refers to his exceptionally lucrative 12-foot land claim where he struck it rich in the Cariboo Gold Rush. He later settled in Peace River.

Opposite bottom right: The Canadian flag proudly adorns a roadside barn.

Top: With Northern Alberta's abundance of game animals and fishing opportunities, hunters and fishermen can have the experience of a lifetime from a remote lodge such as this one.

Bottom: Burnt trees stretch their trunks skywards after a forest fire. Fires occur frequently in Northern Alberta's forests as the result of lightning strikes. Fire has a significant regenerative effect on a forest, creating new foraging grounds for animals and allowing for new growth.

Opposite: Northern Alberta's waterways and forests are among the most pristine left in the world.

Andrew Bradley was born in Melbourne, Australia in 1962. An avid outdoorsman and world traveller, Andrew has spent time in Toronto, Los Angeles and New York. He has lived and worked in his adopted province, Alberta, since 1996. A self-taught photographer, Andrew is also a pilot with an eye for aerial views.